Express Guide

Ubuntu

Desktop

Version 20.04 LTS

Shiv Kumar Goyal

Preface

Welcome to Ubuntu Desktop 20.04. The purpose of writing this book is to help the Ubuntu users in performing day to day tasks on Ubuntu desktop. This book emphasis on practical aspect of Ubuntu desktop therefore you will find procedures with minimal theory.

Enjoy and be happy

Shiv Kumar Goyal

Contents

Chapter 1

Introduction

Linux is an Operating system just like Microsoft Windows and MAC OS. Linux is an open source project started by Linus Torvalds in 1991. Since then Linux has undergone long evolution cycle, from just basic kernel to complete Graphical operating system.

Introduction to Ubuntu

Ubuntu is free to use Linux distribution. Canonical Ltd, owned by South African Entrepreneur Mark Shuttleworth, funded Ubuntu project. On 8 July 2005, Mark Shuttleworth and Canonical announced the creation of the Ubuntu Foundation and provided an initial funding of US$10 million. The main aim of the foundation was to provide funds for future development and promotion of Ubuntu Linux.

Ubuntu is Debian based Linux distribution. Where Debian is another Linux operating system with long development cycle. Ubuntu takes source code from Debian Linux latest unstable branch and adapts them to the Ubuntu. Ubuntu also patches and add additional features to these packages if necessary and then push back these enhancements to Debian developers. Ubuntu comes up with new release after every six months. Every forth release is known as Long Term Support (LTS) version. LTS version receives updates and patches for 5 years. Current LTS version is 20.04 (Code Name **Focal Fossa**). Ubuntu 20.04 LTS will be supported for 5 years until April 2025. Earlier there use to be two versions of Ubuntu on Intel platform i.e. 32 bit and 64 bit. As all latest computers available these days are 64 bit therefore Ubuntu has decided to provide only 64 bit image of Ubuntu.

Chapter 2

New Features in Ubuntu 20.04 LTS

Ubuntu 20.04 has many new features compared to its predecessor versions, following are some of the main new features: -

- New Linux Kernel 5.4.
- Faster boot
- OEM's Logo on the Boot Screen
- New and Improved appearance.
- Dark theme
- Do not disturb option for notifications
- Redesigned login screen
- Fractional scaling setting.
- GNOME 3.36.

Chapter 3

Minimum System Requirement

Following are minimum requirements to install Ubuntu Linux. However, it is ideal to have more resources than this for optimum working of applications.

Processor   1 gigahertz or better

System memory (RAM)   2 GB

Hard disk   10GB

VGA resolution of 1024X 768

Ether **CD/DVD** or **USB** for installer media

Chapter 4

Installation

Ubuntu Desktop installation is very simple and straight forward. The normal installation is good for personal and professional use. Lets start..

Media preparation

1. Open Ubuntu site https://ubuntu.com/download/desktop and press download button, to download ISO file.

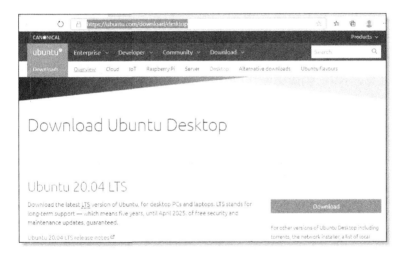

2. Burn the downloaded ISO image file to DVD.

   Or

   Create USB media with following steps

1. For USB preparation, download universal USB installer from
   https://www.pendrivelinux.com/universal-usb-installer-easy-as-1-2-3/

2. Run the downloaded program. And press I agree.
3. Insert USB media.

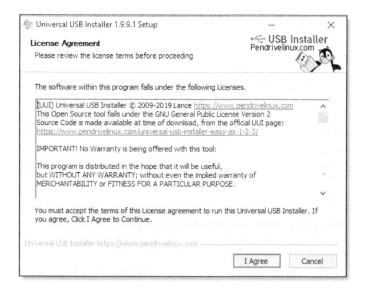

4. On **Setup your Selection Page,** select the **Ubuntu** in **step1** drop down menu

5. In **Step 2,** select the location of the downloaded Ubuntu ISO file.

6. In the **Step 3,** select the USB drive from drop down menu.

7. Press **Create**.

Once USB creation is done, attach USB media to machine where you want to do installation.

Steps for installation

1. Switch on the computer and press appropriate key to change the boot priority like F12 in case of Lenovo laptops. Key for boot menu differs from system to

system, check the system manual for that. Select the USB created in previous step from the list.

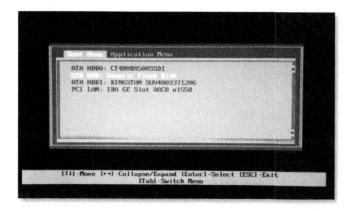

2. On **Installer boot menu**, Select **Install Ubuntu.**

3. Select the language on **Welcome** screen. Press **Continue**.

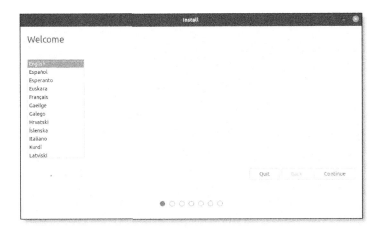

4. Select **keyboard Language and Keyboard layout.**

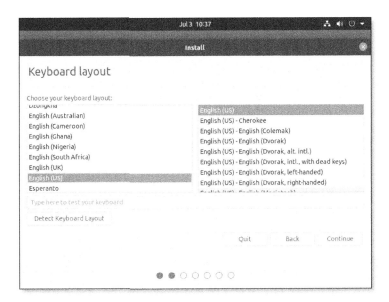

5. Although you can skip this step, but it is ideal to have internet during installation so that system can install third party tools and updates. Select your network from the list and press **Connect.**

9

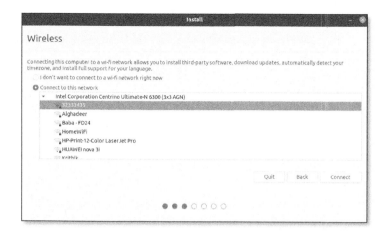

6. If your wireless network is protected by password it will prompt for password. Write password and press **Connect.**

7. In this step select **Normal Installation**. Make Sure these two radio boxes ticked, **Download updates while installing Ubuntu** and **Install third party graphics and Wi-Fi hardware and additional media format**.

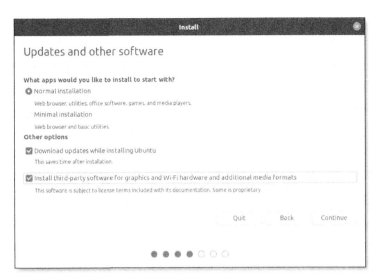

8. Select **Erase disk and install Ubuntu**.

Warning: This step is for fresh hard disk. As this step erase any data present on the system hard disk. If you have any data on the disk, please take backup before performing this task.

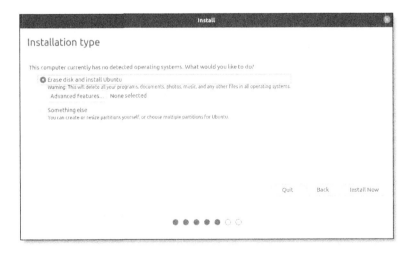

9. Choose preferred Time Zone. If you are connected to internet the system will automatically pick the correct time zone.

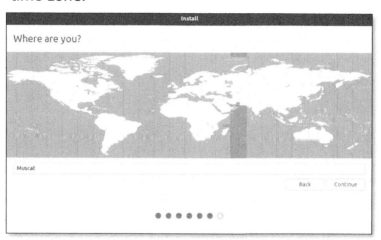

10. Enter **Your name, Computer name and Password.** select **login automatically**. Press **Continue**.

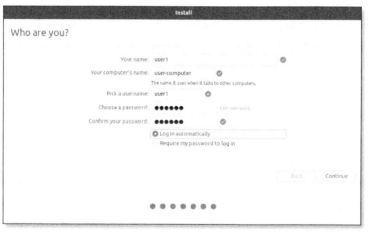

Note: This password is very important This password will be used in all administrative commands.

11. The installation process will start.

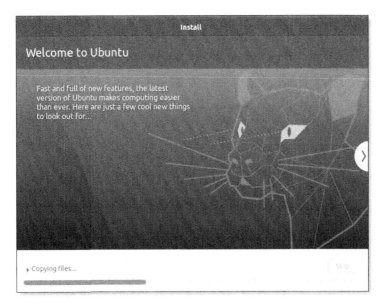

12. Press **Restart** ,on completion of copying process.

Post Installation Steps

1. After System restart, system offers you to connect online account. Press **Skip**.

2. Press Next on **Livepatch** Screen.

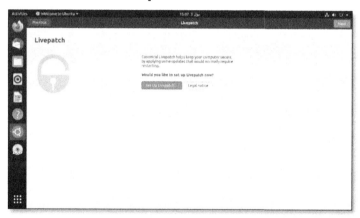

3. Press **Next** on Help improve Ubuntu.

4. Press **Next** on privacy screen.

5. Press **Done**.

This concludes basic installation process of Ubuntu desktop.

Chapter 5

Getting started with the desktop

Gnome is the default desktop environment for Ubuntu 20.04. In this chapter we will explore Ubuntu desktop interfaces

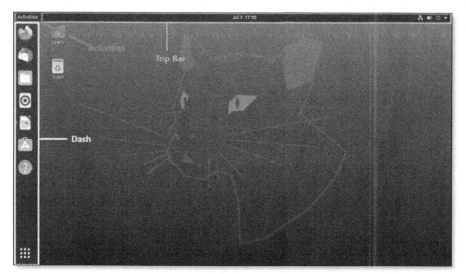

TOP BAR

The top bar has four main sections.

- System Menu
- Clock
- Activities
- Application menu

System Menu

Right corner of the bar has power, speaker network, battery and Bluetooth icons. Click any of these icons to open **System menu**.

System menu allows you to adjust speaker and microphone volume. This menu also give you option to adjust network and Bluetooth settings. You will find quick links for system settings, Lock screen and Shutdown Menu.

Clock

In the center of the bar there is clock and by default it shows day of the week and current time in 24-hour format. If you want, you can change the time format in the system settings. Click clock to open dialog box with calendar on the right side and any task notification on the left side.

Activities

On the left side of the top bar is **Activities** button. Click on this button to open overview screen. You can press Super key (also known as Windows ⊞ key) on your keyboard to open Activities overview.

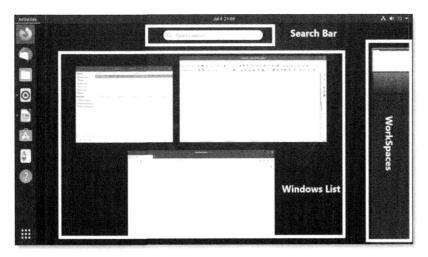

Search Bar

17

One of the main item of Activities overview screen is search bar. With search bar you can search applications, documents, settings, calendar events etc. on your computer. For example, if you write calculator in the search bar it will show calculator application.

Click the icon to open the calculator application.

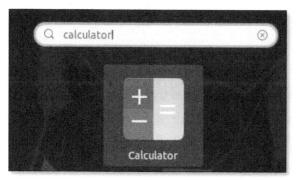

Windows Peak View

Second item of Activity overview is peek view of all running applications. Click the desired application window to switch application. To close any running application window, hover over the window and click X button.

Workspaces

Left side of the Activities overview screen shows the list of workspaces. **Workspaces** are virtual desktops for better windows management. Click on the workspace to switch workspace. To move the application to different workspace just drag the running application to new workspace.

DASH

On the left side of the desktop you will find the dash bar. The **Dash** provides access to your favorite and running applications. Click the application icon on the dash bar to open the application. The small dot on the left side of icon indicates running application. Click on any running application icon brings most recent window of the application. Right click on the icon to open context menu. From this menu

you can open new window or pick any window of a running application. You can also add or remove any application to favorites from this menu.

19

Grid

At the bottom of the dash bar there is grid icon. Click on this icon shows the list of all and frequently used applications. The icons are in grid format, from the bottom of the grid you can switch between all applications and frequently used applications. The list of applications can span multiple pages, to navigate to next page use scroll (center) wheel of mouse or click the dots on the right side of the grid.

Some applications in the grid are contained in the application folder. Click application folder to list the grid of all containing applications.

Application menu

Located beside the Activities button, application menu shows the name of the active application. Also provides other options specific to the active application.

System setting.

Click on system setting icon in the system menu will open settings windows for system and hardware. Setting screen has two panes, left pane shows the list of settings and right pane

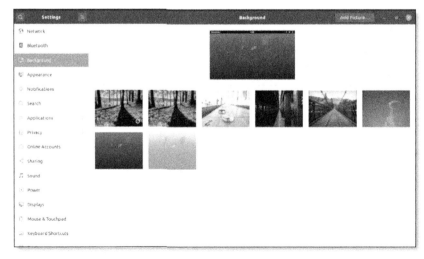

provides the description of the selected setting. You can scroll the list of settings with mouse's scroll wheel. Suppose you want to change the background of your desktop. Click background in the left pane and select the wallpaper from the list of available wallpapers in the right pane.

Top bar of the system setting tool also houses search button. Search button offers you to search anything related to settings. Suppose to look for date and time settings just press search button and write date. The system will show you list of items related to date in the left pane.

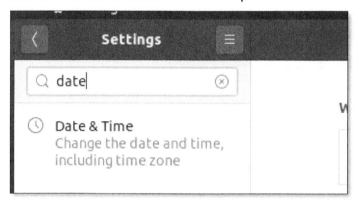

Log out or switch user

Ubuntu provides you option to share your computer with other users. To let other users use your computer either you press Logout or Switch user. When you pick **Logout** all your running application will close, on the other hand when you press **Switch user** all your applications will continue running, and everything will be same when you log back.

To Logout or Switch user, click **Power Off/ Log Out** and then pick the option you want.

Lock screen

When you are away from your machine for short time it is recommended to lock your screen so nobody can use your computer in your absence. When system screen is in lock state, all the running application will continue running. To log back, provide your login password to unlock the screen. System also locks the screen automatically, if you leave your computer for a specific time period.

To lock the screen manually, click the system menu on the right side of the top bar, click **Lock** option.

To unlock, press ENTER key on the locked screen and provide your password.

Suspend

Ubuntu automatically changes the system to suspend mode when you close the lid of your laptop. In the suspend mode system uses very less power to save energy. All your applications keep running in suspend mode, but screen and other non-essential parts of the computer switch off to save power.

To change the system to suspend mode, click the system menu on the right side of the top bar, click **Power Off/ Log Out** option to open collapsed menu and pick **Suspend** option.

Power off or Restart

To switch off your computer or to restart the whole computer, click the system menu on the right side of the top bar, click **Power Off/ Log Out option** to open collapsed menu and then choose the **Power Off** option. A dialog box will open, press the button you want.

Power Off		
The system will power off automatically in 60 seconds.		
Cancel	Restart	Power Off

Windows

Ubuntu uses windows to display your running applications. This is one of the way to run multiple tasks at same time. Whenever you launch any application it opens in new window. In this section we will explore windows.

List windows

To see all running windows just click **Activities** button. From the list of windows press left button of mouse to select the window.

Switch window

You can switch the window using key board, press Super key + TAB to open windows switcher.

Hold Super key, release and press TAB key to cycle between open windows.

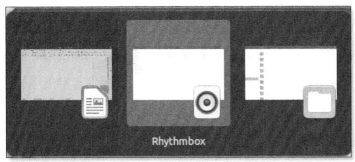

| **Please note**: ▦ key on your keyboard is referred as super key |

Maximize and unmaximize a window

You can maximize a window to see the content of windows on whole desktop and unmaximize or restore down a window to restore it to its normal size.

Maximize the Window

To maximize a window, press and hold left button of mouse at title bar of the window to grab the window title bar, now drag it to the top bar. Other way is to double click left button of mouse on the title bar of window. To maximize a window using the keyboard press Alt + F10 . You can also press maximize button on the window's title bar to maximize the window.

Unmaximize window

To restore a window to its normal size grab the window title bar and drag away from the top bar or just double click title bar of window.   Press Alt + F10 on the key board to unmaximize the windows using keyboard. Another way to unmaximize is to press unmaximize button on the window's title bar.

Tile Windows (Snap Windows)

To copy files or to compare content of two windows you can place two windows side-by-side. In Microsoft windows this feature is known as windows Snap. To snap window to left side press Super + left Arrow and to snap window right side of screen select the window, press Super + right arrow key on the keyboard. To snap window using mouse grab the title of window and drag it to the left or right side until half of the screen is highlighted.

Switch workspaces

Workspaces are virtual desktops. It is like having more than one monitors virtually on same desktop. If you are working on several applications at same time, workspace is good option to organize them. To move one application from current workspace to another workspace, press **Activities** to view the

list of windows and workspaces. Grab the title of widow and

move to new workspace from the list of workspaces on right side of screen.

To move to a workspace, Click **Activities** and select the workspace or press Super + Page Down and Super + Page Up on your keyboard.

Chapter 6

Update Ubuntu

The updates contain important bug fixes, security patches and new features. To improve the performance, stability and security of the operating system and applications on your computer system need to be updated regularly. Installing them ensures that your system runs safely and efficiently. Ubuntu has a mechanism for automatic check for updates. If you want to do manual update, you can do this using graphical user interface. It is a good idea to update the system after fresh installation. To check new updates:

1. Click **Activities**.
2. In the search bar write update. Click on **Software updates icon**.

3. It will open dialog box like bellow.

4. Press **Install Now**, if any new updates are available.

5. At password prompt, provide password you selected at installation time and press **Authenticate**.

6. This will start update process.

7. Some updates require system restart, press **Restart Now,** if prompted**.**

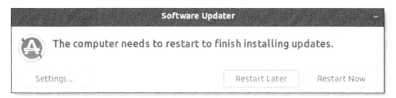

This completes system update process. in future if system prompts you to install the updates, follow the procedure from step 4 onward.

Chapter 7

Personalize your desktop

Ubuntu Desktop makes it easy to customize the look and feel of your desktop. You can personalize your desktop according to your taste and comfort. We will change list of settings to personalize your desktop. It is not mandatory to change all settings.

Change the background.

    1. Open settings from system menu.

    2. In the left pane select background.

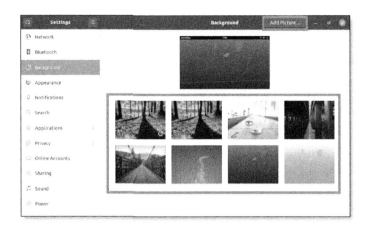

3. Click any picture from the list in the right pane to set it as wallpaper (background of your desktop).

4. To use your own image as background click **Add picture**.

5. User's picture folder will open. Select the picture and press open.

6. Click the newly added image to set as background.

Change system theme

One of the new feature in the Ubuntu 20.04 is dark theme. Other than dark theme two more themes are light and standard. To change the color theme of the system.

1. Click **Appearance** in the left pane of the setting window.

2. Select the theme under **Windows colors** section.

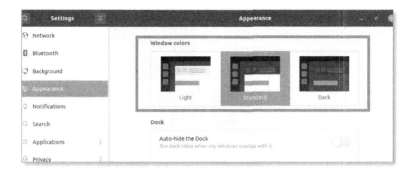

Customize Dash

To customize the appearance of dash bar. Open the settings and select the appearance in the left pane.   Under Dock heading you can change following settings

1. **Auto-hide the dock**: Automatically hide the dash bar when window is in maximized form to use maximum real estate of the screen.

2. **Icon Size:** By default, the size of dash bar is 48, if that's too big or too small for your screen you can change the size by moving the slider to left or right. When you move left the size will decrease and on right side the size will increase.

3. **Position on screen**: To change the position of dash bar on the screen select option from the drop down menu.

Change alert sound

For every message or event system plays a sound to alert you. To change the alert sound.

1. In the setting window select Sound on the left pane.
2. Under the alert section on the right pane, select the sound you like.

Change Screen privacy

Automatic screen Blank

For your privacy the screen goes blank when you don't use your computer for certain period of time. You can change this settings:-

1. Click **Privacy** on left pane in the setting window.
2. Select **Screen lock**.
3. On the right pane you can change the duration after which the screen will go blank from the drop down menu between 1 minute to 15 minutes.

4. To disable screen blank feature, select Never from the drop down menu.

Automatic screen lock

Automatic screen lock is a feature for security and privacy of your system. The screen gets lock after certain period of inactivity on the computer. To unlock the screen, you need to enter your login password. To change the Automatic screen lock behavior:-

On the screen lock pane in the setting window change the following settings

1. **Automatic Screen lock:** Slide the button to right side to enable automatic screen lock.

2. **Automatic screen lock delay:** Select the duration of inactivity from 30 second to 1 hour using dropdown menu.

Chapter 8

Change date, time and timezone

Date and time are very important settings of any computer system. Many functions such as automated backups, system logs depend on time and date. In the center of the top bar there is clock which shows time and date. If date and time on this clock is incorrect or in wrong format, you can change that using following procedure:

1. Click **Setting** from the system menu.
2. In the setting window select **Date and time** in the left pane.

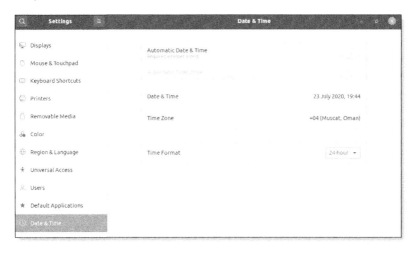

3. Change **Automatic Date & Time** switch to off position, to update your date and time manually. When this button is in on position, system updates time from internet automatically.

4. Click **Date & Time** and then adjust the time and date.

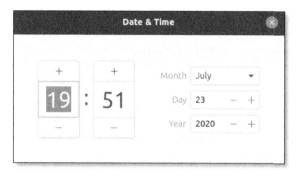

5. You can click **Time zone** to adjust time zone if the present time zone is not correct. To change the time zone click your present country on the map.

6. If required change **Time Format** from 24-hour to AM/PM or vice versa using dropdown menu.

Chapter 9

Manage Users

As Linux is a multi-user operating system, it allows multiple users to access the same system. You can create separate user account for each user of computer so that every user can keep his or her data separate and safe. This provides privacy to the all users. User can also personalize the desktop according his or her taste.

What is User

A **user** is anyone who uses a computer. Linux assign unique user id to every user that exists on system which in known as UID or User ID. This UID is for systems internal use only.

Standard v/s Administrator

The administrator is special user who has complete access to the operating system and its configuration. The administrator user is intended for administrative use only. In traditional Unix systems there use to be **root** user for doing administrative task. Administrator user has unlimited privileges. Administrator can access any file, run any program, execute any system call, and modify any setting. Unlike standard user Administrator can access the files and folders of other users also. During the installation, system creates administrator user. When you create new user you have option to select Standard or administrator as user account type.

Add User

To create user

1. From system menu press **Settings**.

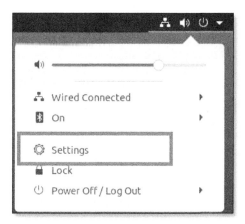

2. In the setting windows on left pane select **Users**.

3. Press **unlock**. Provide password and press **Authenticate**.

4. Press **Add User.**

5. In the **Add User** dialog box do following :

   1. Select type of user as **Standard** or **Administrator**.

   2. Write the **Full name** of the user
   3. Change the system generated username if required.

4. For **Password,** either you can set password now or allow user to set password on first login.

5. Press **Add**.

6. List of users at the top will show new user.

7. To test this user, click System menu, click **Power off/Logout** and press **LogOut**

8. At login screen, select the user and provide password. Press Enter key.

   If you had selected **Allow user to set a password when they next login**, then provide new password and press Enter key. Type same password again followed by Enter key.

9. After login follow the post installation steps.

Modify user

To change the property of any user you have to use administrator user account like the one we created at the time of installation.

1. To modify any user first unlock the user settings, press **Unlock** button. Provide password and press **Authenticate**.

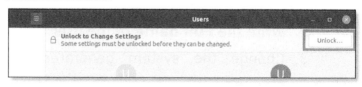

2. Select the user.

3. Press pencil icon to modify full name.

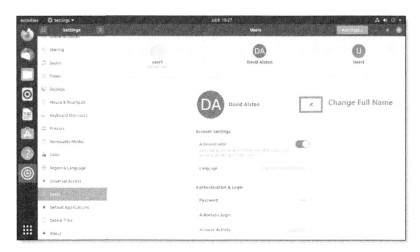

4. User type slide button let you modify account type from Standard to Administrator and vice versa.

5. To change language for the user, press greater then sign.

Under **Authentication & login** you can change

- Password
- **Automatic Login**. Make user account to login automatically without password prompt at system start.
- **Account activity** press greater than sign to display user's login history.

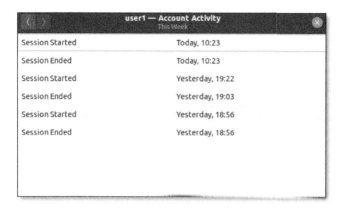

Remove user

If situation arises that any user account is no more required, you can easily delete the user.

1. Open User setting
2. Press **Unlock**.
3. Select the user for deletion.
4. At bottom of the user screen you will see Remove User button, press the button.

At dialog box for confirmation to delete or keep the user's files, press appropriate button.

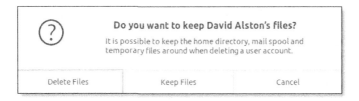

Chapter 10

Manage files and folders

Linux stores data in files. All files are organized into folders. Folders can have sub folders. These folders are organized into a tree-like structure known as filesystem.

Folders

All the files, whether data, program, or folder, are contained in folders. Folder also known as directory is way to organize files. These folders may have sub folders and further sub folder.

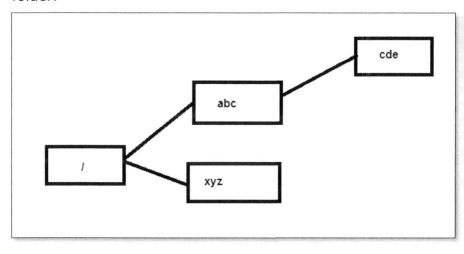

In this example, abc and xyz are folders on root and cde is sub folder under abc. To represent abc and xyz we will write

/abc and /xyz respectively. To represent cde we will write /abc/cde.

Path

Path is location of file or folder.

Home folder

In a multi user environment every user has his own home folder. The home folder holds user's personnel files including documents, pictures, music and videos.

Files, The file manager for Ubuntu

Ubuntu provides **Files** as the file manager for exploring files and folders on your computer. and on external storage devices like external hard disks, USB drive or DVDROM. File manager can also explore files on remote file servers and network shares.

To open file manager, click files icon on the dash bar or write files in search bar.

Basics of File manager

The file manager has two panes, the left is a side bar (bookmark bar) and the right pane is main view area. On the left side of top bar starts with back (less then sign) and forward (greater then sign) buttons. Next on top bar is the path. Search sign is to search files and folders.

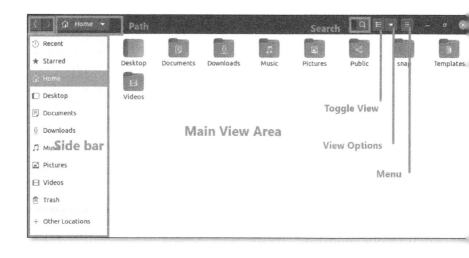

Exploring the contents of folders

Double-click any folder in the main view area to list its contents. To open any file either double click the file or press middle wheal button of your mouse. To go back to previous location either click the back button from top bar or click the location folder from the path bar. File manager furthermore provides tab view to manage files and folders. To open folder in the new tab press middle button of mouse or right click on the folder and select **open in new tab**. You can also right-click a folder to open it in a new window. Press search icon to find any file or folder.

Side bar is a favorite bar which shows bookmarks like documents, desktop, music, picture etc. You can also add your own frequently used folders as bookmark in the side bar. To add your folder as bookmark, drag the folder to the sidebar, and drop it over **New bookmark**, which appears dynamically.

Otherwise click the folder in the path bar and select **Add to Bookmarks**.

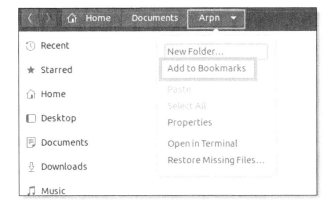

Context menu

Right click of mouse on any file or folder shows context menu. From this context menu you can perform various tasks like rename, copy, paste and move to trash etc. Being a context menu it varies according to the selected object.

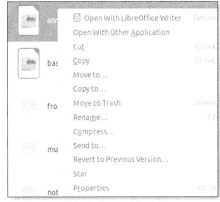

Rename a file or folder

To change the name of file or folder. Right click the folder or file and select **Rename** from the context menu. Rename the file or folder using keyboard, select file or folder and press F2 key from the keyboard.

Write the new name of file or folder in the dialog box and press **Rename**.

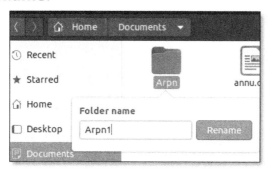

Copy

There are multiple ways to copy file.

Using mouse

1. Right click the file or folder you want to copy.

2. From the context menu select **Copy.**

3. Now open the target folder where you want to copy the file or folder.

4. Right click and select **Paste** from the context menu.

Using keyboard.

1. Select the file or folder you want copy.

2. Press Ctrl + C key to copy.

3. Open the target folder.

4. Press Ctrl + V key to paste

Move file or folder.

To move file or folder.

Using mouse

1. Right click on the file or folder to move and select **Cut.**

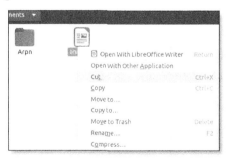

2. Open the target location.

3. Right click on mouse and select **Paste** from the context menu.

Using Keyboard

1. Select the file or folder you want move.

2. Press $\boxed{\text{Ctrl}}$ + $\boxed{\text{X}}$ key to cut.

3. Open the target folder.

4. Press $\boxed{\text{Ctrl}}$ + $\boxed{\text{V}}$ key to paste

Drag and drop to copy or move files

To copy file from one source to target using drag and drop.

1. Open the source folder.

2. Press $\boxed{\text{Ctrl}}$ + $\boxed{\text{N}}$ from the key board to open new windows or open the file menu and select new window.

3. Open the target folder in the new window.

4. Unmaximize the new window.

5. Go to the previous window

6. Press and hold left button of mouse and Ctrl key on keyboard. Drag the file or folder to target window and release both buttons at target.

Do not press Ctrl key while dragging to move the file or folder.

Delete

If the file or folder is no more required, you can delete it to free up the space on the disk.

1. Select the file or folder to delete.
2. Right click on the mouse and select **Move to Trash** from the context menu.

   Or

   Press Delete key from the keyboard.

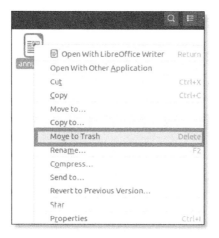

It will move the files to trash. The files in trash can be restored if deleted by mistake.

Empty Trash

To reclaim the space of deleted files:-

1. Right click on the trash icon on the left pane.
2. Select **Empty Trash** from context menu.

3. Press **Empty Trash** on confirmation popup.

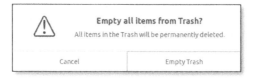

To delete the file permanently without moving to trash

1. Select the file or folder you want to delete.

2. Press and hold $\boxed{\text{Shift}}$ key and press $\boxed{\text{Delete}}$ key on your keyboard.

It will prompt for confirmation press Delete button.

Change view

By default, file manager shows files and folder in icon view. To change the view to list view and vice versa press toggle view button on the top bar of the file manager.

Sort

To sort the list of files and folder.

1. Toggle the view to list view.

2. It will show columns with more attributes. Click heading of the column to sort the list Press same heading again to sort the view in reverse order.

Chapter 11

Automated Backup

Backup consist of three W's, **W**hat **W**here and **W**hen.

What

First thing you have to decide **what** is the most important part of the data which you want to keep safe. Generally, documents and pictures are most important part of the data. Music, movies and downloads can be less important.

Where

Where to keep the backup? Backup on the same hard drive will save you from accidental deletion and corruption, but not in case of drive failure and viruses. Second option to store backup is external storage like USB and external hard drive. Cloud storage in another good option as Ubuntu support both google and next cloud.

When

Third most important part of backup planning is frequency of backup. Frequency of backup normally depends upon frequency of data change on your computer.

Now you have answer of all three W's, lets configure backup.

1. Press **Activities**
2. In the search box write Backups
3. Click the **Backups** Icon.

Configure Backup

Ubuntu uses Deja Dup as default backup tool. To configure automatic backup follow these steps:-

Press **enable** link in the right pane to configure the backups.

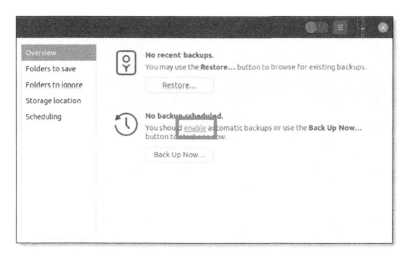

It will prompt you to install additional packages, press **Install** button.

This will configure the backup with default options.

Customize

To customize backup, click the items in left pane one by one.

Folders to save

This tab defines which items will be saved as backup. By default, your whole home directory is selected for backup. If you want to add some other folder press **+** button at the bottom. To remove the existing folder use **-** button.

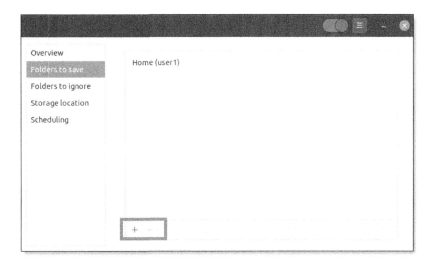

Folder to ignore

This field defines list of folders to be excluded from the backup. In the right pane it shows all folders to be excluded, press **+** button to add more and **-** to remove existing. By default, download and trash folder is excluded from backup.

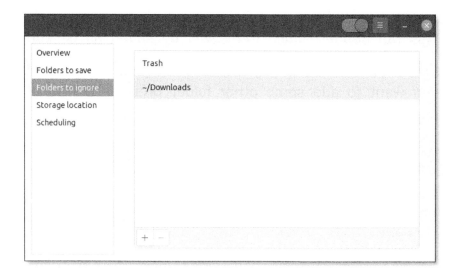

Storage location

Storage location specify the target location for backup. As mentioned you should select external storage or cloud. Beware, when you use external media for automatic backup it should be connected at the time of backup. Use drop down menu to set the **Storage location.**

Scheduling tab

Now press **Scheduling** to change the schedule of backup. On this screen you have three options. Use slide button to switch On/Off Automatic backup. **Every** drop down menu is to set the frequency of backup, it can be weekly, daily. Third thing is retention period of backup under **Keep** drop down menu.

Test the backup

To take manual backup go to overview tab and press **Backup now**. If you use this first time configuration window will appear. Select **Password-protect your backup** to ensure that no one can access your backup without password. Press **Forward** to start backup.

Restore Backup

In case of data loss due to any reason like hard disk crash or virus you may require to restore backup.

1. Open backups
2. On **Overview** screen press **Restore**.

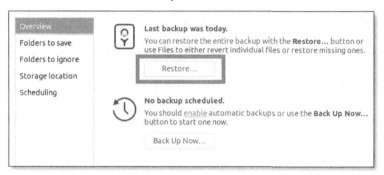

3. To select the source of backup to restore, pick the device from the drop down list. Select the **Folder** of backup. Press **Forward** button.

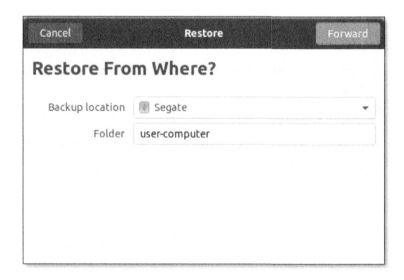

4. As same location may contain multiple backups for different dates, select the date of backup you want to restore. Press **Forward** button.

5. When you restore the backup you can restore the backup at original location or at different location. Select different location to avoid replacing updated files. Press **Forward**.

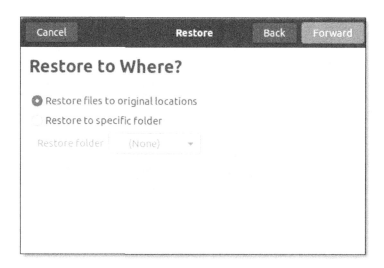

6. Next screen shows summary, if you are happy with the configuration press **Restore**.

7. Press **Close**.

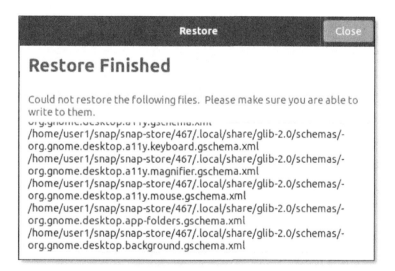

Chapter 12

Email

Thunderbird is default email client in Ubuntu. Thunderbird allows users to send, receive Email. Thunderbird is a lightweight mail client supports different mail accounts POP, IMAP, Gmail etc. Best part of the email client is that you can read and write the emails offline.

Open email client Thunderbird.

Click Thunderbird icon on the Dash bar or press **Activities**
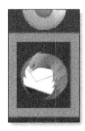 button and write email and click Thunderbird icon. The setup window will open when you start first time.

Configure Thunderbird

Enter the Following details on the first screen

- Full name
- Email address
- Password to access email address.
- Make sure **Remember password** is checked, so you don't have to re-enter password each time.

Press **Continue**

On the next screen it will try to configure the email client automatically, if thunderbird has configuration of Email provider in its database.

If you are using Other account which thunderbird is not able to configure automatically you can press **Manual config** and provide server configuration. In this example we will configure Gmail email account for pop3 access. Check your service provide for email client configuration.

In the next screen, select whether you want to use POP3 or IMAP. Press **Done**.

Click **Inbox** in the left pane to see your emails

Problem with GMAIL account configuration.

If you face following error while configuring: -

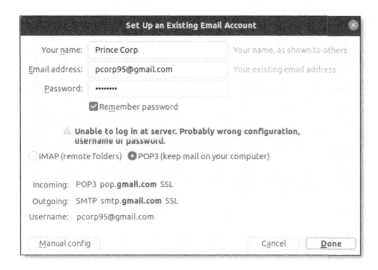

Login to Gmail account in the web browser and change your account security setting ,**Allow less secure apps to ON**

Write Email

Press Write button to create email.

It will open interface for writing mail.

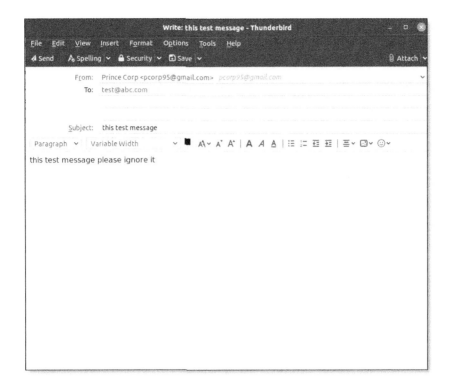

After writing email. Press **Send**.

Extra configuration for Gmail account

If you are using Gmail account and try to send mail first time authentication screen for google account will popup. Provide password of Gmail account and press Sign-in

On next screen press **Allow.** This will allow you send mails from Thunderbird. This step is required only first time for Gmail account.

Check for new Messages.

Thunderbird checks new messages at start and after regular intervals. To check new messages manually, Press **Get Messages**.

Change Theme of Thunderbird

Advantage of the open source software is ability to customize..
To change look(theme) of Thunderbird:-

Click button. Select **Add-ons**.

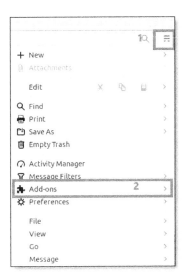

Press Enable button to switch theme. If you like dark interface press Enable button against Dark theme.

You can add more themes write the name of the theme in the search bar and press Enter key. Press **Add to Thunderbird** from the list of the themes.

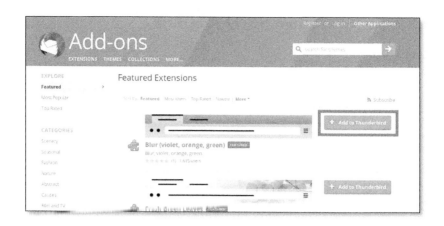

Chapter 13

Removable media

USB Drives and external hard drives are great for storing files and sharing files. Not only these storages are great for storage of data but also good for backup. USB and external storage provides mobility and flexibility.

Use the USB Drive / External hard drive

Copy Files

1.   Plugin in the drive in your computer.

2.   Drive might automatically open in new windows, if not click the drive icon on the left side dash bar. Now new windows will appear for USB drive / External HDD folder. Unmaximize(Restore down) the window using button [ ] on the top bar of the window.

3.   Open the new window as source of the files you want to copy. Unmaximize (restore down) this window also using [ ] .

There are multiple ways to store the files on USB drive.

Drag and drop

First select the files with mouse and drag down to USB drive window to copy files.

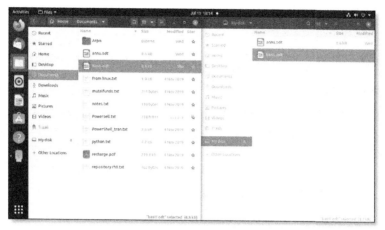

You can also copy files by dragging files to USB icon under devices on the left pan.

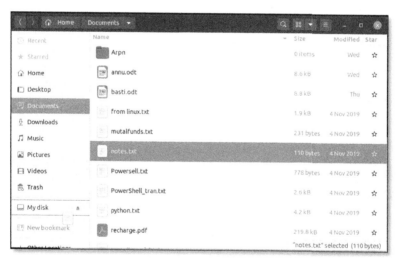

Copy and paste

Copy paste is another way to save files to USB drive.

Select the files using right click of the mouse and select **copy** commands from the context menu.

Now on the USB drive folder right click again and this time select **Paste** from the menu.

Save As

To save files when working in the application.

Suppose you are working in libre Writer. Click **File** menu and select **Save As**.

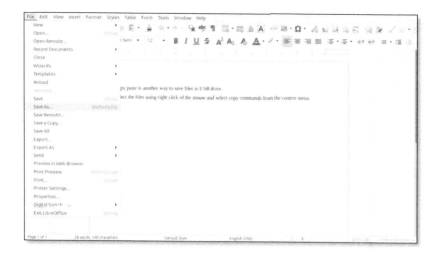

Now go to the USB drive and press save. If required change the name of file.

Delete files

To delete the files from USB to free up the space. Just right click on file and select Move to trash.

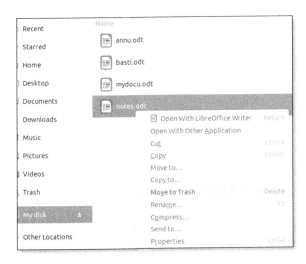

Once the file is in trash empty the trash press right click and select **Empty trash** on the trash icon to free up the space in the drive.

Alternatively, you drag the file straight to the trash can. Empty trash.

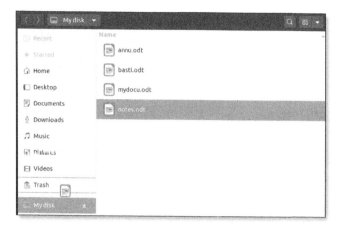

Formatting the USB Drive

Formatting is great tool to achieve following goals: -

- Empty USB drive.
- It is also useful to make USB drive compatible with other operating systems

Please note: - The formatting process erases all data from your disk so make sure there is no important data already there on the USB drive.

To format the drive

1. Press **Activities**.
2. In the search bar write **Disks**.

3. Select the **Disks** icon.

4. In the disk interface select the USB drive from the left pane.

5. Press umount button from the right pane.

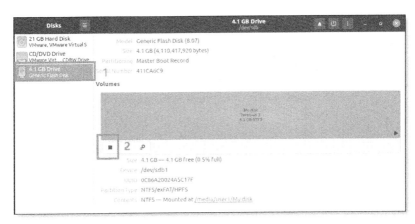

6. Click gear icon it will present sub menu. From menu select **Format Partition.**

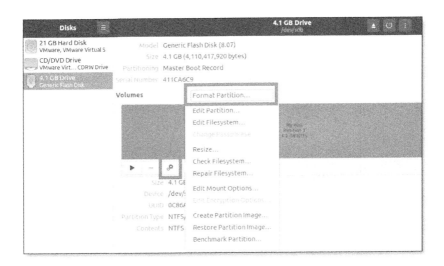

7. In the format window you can change type of the file system and name of device. Click **Next**

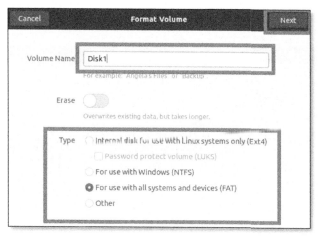

8. Click **Format** in the confirm details window.

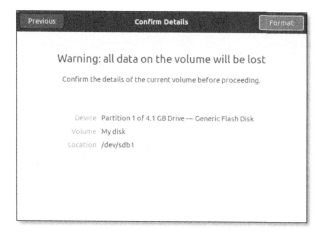

Eject The USB drive.

Before removing the USB drive from the system make sure you **Eject** the drive to ensure that the drive is no longer being used. Removing drive without proper Eject can cause data corruption. Right click on the drive icon on the dash bar and select **Eject** from the context menu. When icon vanishes you are free to remove the USB drive from the system.

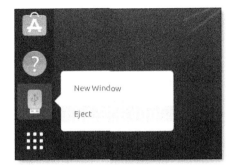

Chapter 14

Network

What is computer Network

A computer network is group of computers and computing devices that arc linked together. This link provides communication between the different computers and devices in that group. Computer and devices can use wire, fiber optic or microwave as a medium of communication. There are many types of networks, but we will focus on TCP/IP as it is the most popular suite in use both in Local Area Network (LAN) and Wide Area Network (WAN) such as internet.

On personal computer network is generally used for connecting internet or sharing files and printers. On Ubuntu desktop normally you use two types of networks connections. Network connectivity can be either wired or wireless i.e Wi-Fi. We will discuss both type of networking. In Linux we call each computer as host.

Connecting Wireless connection.

When your wireless network is connected it will show Wi-Fi 🛜 icon on the top bar. If you don't see this icon this means you are not connected to wireless network. To connect to your home or office wireless network follow bellow procedure

1. Click system menu.
2. Click **Wireless not connected** to expand collapsed menu.

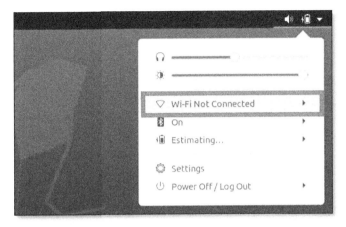

3. Click select network.

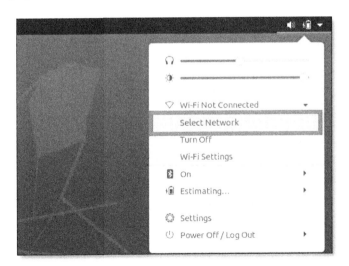

4. New screen will open with all available networks. Select your Wi-Fi network name. Press **Connect**.

5. If network is password protected it will ask for password. Provide password and press **Connect**.

6. Now your network is connected and top bar will show Wi-Fi icon.

Change Wi-Fi Password

If for some reasons you had changed the Wi-Fi network password on your Wi-Fi router, you have to set the same password in your system also otherwise, it will not connect.

1. Click System menu.
2. Click wireless Connected to open sub menu.
3. Click change settings
4. From the list of available networks select your network and press gear icon next to it.
5. In security setting change password and press ok.

Wired network

Connecting wired network is easy, just plug the network cable to your computer. The system will automatically configure the system for available network. As soon as system connects to wired network system indicator shows on top bar.

Manual Wired network configuration.

Most of the time wired network setting is automatic, but in some cases you have to set IP address manually. This type of configuration is known as static IP address configuration.

To configure static IP address:-

1. Open System Menu.
2. Click **Wired Connected**.
3. It will expand the menu.

4. Click **Wired settings.**

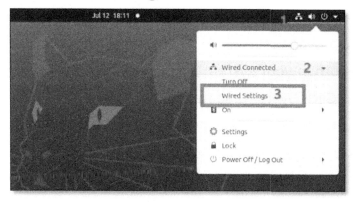

5. It will bring Network settings windows.
6. Wired field shows the status of network like **Connected** click gear icon.

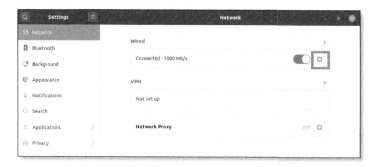

7. Wired profile dialog box will open.
8. In the Details tab make sure **Connect automatically** is ticked.

9. Click **IPv4** tab to set the IP address, click **Manual** radio button.

10. Provide IP address, Netmask, gateway and DNS in the respective fields. Press **Apply**.

Chapter 15

Application management

Ubuntu is open source operating system which provides gateway to wide collection of software which are mostly free to use. Different companies who share these software have different type of terms to use, also known as license. A storage location for these software packages is known as software **repository**. Ubuntu categorize the repositories mainly into four types based on the software license. To install any new software or update installed one, you connect to these repositories available over the internet.

There are many ways to manage the software on Ubuntu, the easiest way is software center. Ubuntu software Center or just Ubuntu Software is a graphical tool to manage software on Ubuntu. With Ubuntu software center you can install, remove and update the software. It also offers you purchase paid software.

Launch Ubuntu Software Center

 Click the Ubuntu Software icon at the Dock bar or click **Activities** and write software in the search bar.

Interface

In the center of top bar there are three tabs **Explore, Installed** and **Updates**. **Explore** tab shows the list of all available software arranged in categories. **Installed** tab shows the list of all currently installed software on your computer. **Updates** tab shows list of any updates available for the software currently installed on the computer.

Install Software

Install using category

The Explore tab shows software arranged in categories. You can click any category to explore the list of available software. Suppose you click Arts and design, it will show all software related to painting, drawing and photography.

1. Click the required software from the list and press **Install** on the software discription screen.

2. On Authentication screen provide password and press **Authenticate**.

The progress bar shows the percentage of completion.

Search and install

If you know the name of software to install, search is the best way to install the software.

On the first screen press search 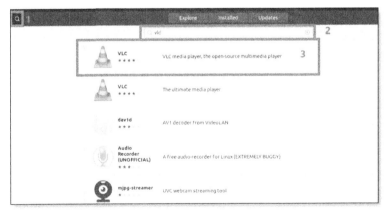 icon. In the search bar write the name of software you want to install. Suppose you want to install VLC player. which is a very popular audio video player.

1. Write vlc in the search bar.
2. From the list of software. Click the software to install.

3. On the software description screen. Press **Install**.

4. Provide password and press **Authenticate** on authentication screen.

5. Installation process will start. The progress bar will display the installation progress.

Remove installed sofware.

At some point of time you may require to delete the installed application to free up the space on the disk. To remove the installed application, open Ubuntu software center.

1. In the search bar write the name of the software you want to remove. For example, you want to remove inkscape installed in the earlier segment. Write inkscape in the search bar. From the list look for required software name and **installed** written in the row.

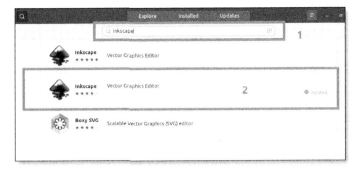

Click the installed software row from the list.

2. On software description screen press remove button.

3. Press Remove at **confirmation** popup.

4. This process requires authentication, provide password and press **Authenticate**. The removal process will start. On completion of removal process remove button will convert to install button on the application description screen.

Chapter 16

Listen music

The default music app in Ubuntu is Rhythmbox. The icon of the Rhythmbox is included on the Dash Bar. Rhythmbox let you play music, listen to podcast and internet radio. To open music player just click the Rhythmbox icon on the dash.

If icon is missing on the dash bar, click **Activities** and in search bar write music and select the Rhythmbox icon

Interface

you will see category in the left pane. Right pane shows list. You can change the view of right pane using tab on the top.

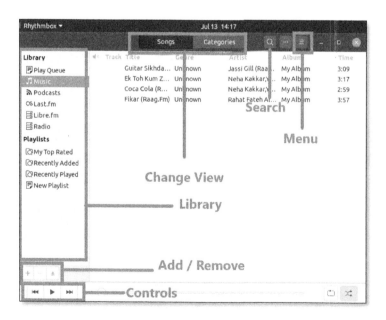

Menu button provides you option to change the view and preferences of Rhythmbox like visible columns, tracks crossfade features etc.

Any music files kept in the user's music folder automatically adds to the playlist of the music player. To change the default location of music library, modify Library location in the preferences of RhythmBox.

Create playlist

Right click on the selected track and click **Add to new playlist**. Type the name for the new playlist and press Enter.

Add songs to play list.

Just drag the song to the play list.

Or

Right click on the selected track or tracks, select Add to Playlist. Select the playlist from the list

Controls

To play song either double click on the song or select the song and press play button on controls at the bottom of the Rhythmbox.

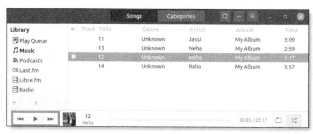

You will see same controls in the notification area to play pause and skip.

Change properties of track

You can edit the properties of song album like artist name, album, composer etc. To change the property, right click on selected track and select properties from context menu. Change required fields in the properties window and press close button. You can also change properties of multiple tracks. To select multiple tracks, use Shift key of keyboard at the time of selection. Right click the selected tracks and select properties.

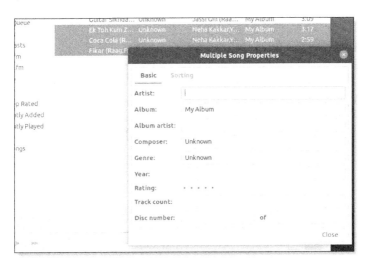

Chapter 17

Play video

Ubuntu comes with video player app known as video. To play any video just double click on it. In this chapter we will discuss another versatile app for video and audio playing. This app is VLC player which we had installed earlier in this book. The VLC is very popular app. One of the main reason for its wide use is ability to play almost all type audio and video formats. The interface of VLC is very much straight forward. If you face problem in playing any audio and video with other app you can try with VLC. There are two ways to play video with VLC.

1. Open the folder in the file manager. Right click on the video file and select **Open with other application**.

2. Choose VLC media player from the list and press **Select**.

Second option open VLC and select video inside VLC.

1. Press **Activities**.

2. In the serach bar write VLC. Click VLC icon.

Click **Media** and select **Open file**. Browse to the folder and select file and press open.

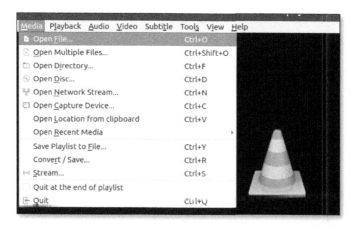

Chapter 18

Photos

The enormous growth in popularity of smartphones and digital cameras has opened a new world of digital photographs. Like physical photographs, digital photographs also require proper management and organization. Shotwell is a digital photo organizer available with Ubuntu desktop environment. It allows you to import photos from disk or camera. Shotwell allows you to organize these photographs and view them in full screen mode. If required, you can also export here photos. To open Shotwell, press **Activities**. In the search bar write photo and click Shotwell icon.

When you start Shotwell it automatically imports any photos in the user's picture folder. You can also import pictures from other folders like in the USB drive, external hard drive or SD card. To import photos from other folder, click **File** and select **Import from folder** and browse to the folder. Press Ok.

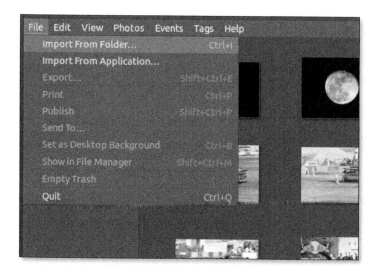

It will prompt you whether you want to **Copy Photos** to library or just **Import in Place**. If you select **Import in Place**, the picture will not be available if source storage is unavailable like removable media.

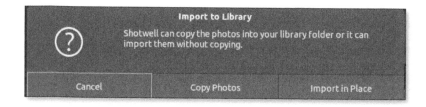

In left pane it shows Events based on meta data of the pictures.

Click the photograph and press F11 key to view in full screen mode. Press F11 again to exit full screen mode. Shotwell also offer some basic tools at bottom bar to manipulate the photos like red eye reduction straighten, rotate and enhancement. Select the picture and click the button at the bottom to adjust the settings.

For photography enthusiasts the metadata of picture like shutter speed, ISO, aperture and other details are available at the bottom of left pane.

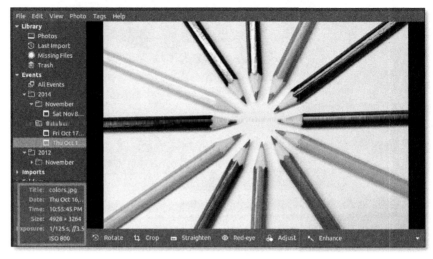

Chapter 19

Download and install Applications

There are many applications which are not available in software center due to license policy. To install this type of application you can download it directly from the site and install it. In this example we will download most popular web browser Google Chrome and install it.

1. Open Mozilla Firefox web browser. To open Firefox, click icon on the dash bar.

2. Write https://www.google.com/chrome/ in the Firefox address and press Enter .

3. Press **Download Chrome**.

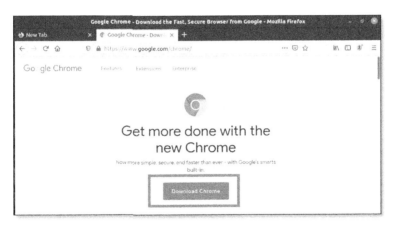

4. Press **Accept and Install**. Download process will start.

5. Select **Save File** and press **OK** button.

6. Go to download folder and double click google-chrome-stable_current_amd64.deb.

7. Software center will open. Press **install** button.

8. Authenticate with password.

9. After completion of installation process, close the software center.

10.Press **Activities** and in the search bar write chrome. Click Google Chrome icon.

11.Once chrome opens, in the dash bar right click on Chrome icon and select **Add to favorite**. So next time you can click Google chrome icon from dash.

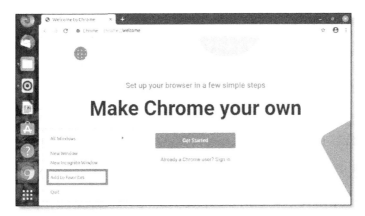

Chapter 20

Write documents

Ubuntu is a complete desktop environment that provides almost all tools required for day to day tasks. For documents it provides LibreOffice as full office suite. Unlike Microsoft office LibreOffice free and open source suite. LibreOffice consist of following applications: -

LibreOffice	Use	MS office
Writer	Word processing	Word
Calc	Spreadsheets	Excel
Impress	Presentations	Power Point
Draw	Vector Graphics and flowcharts	Publisher

Customize the LibreOffice

If you are migrating from MS word to LibreOffice Writer, you can customize the writer to make you feel home.

Install Microsoft fonts

For better compatibility with other Office suite on MS windows it is better to install Microsoft common fonts:-

Open Terminal window using Ctrl + Alt + T keys on the key board or Press Activities and in search bar Write terminal and click the terminal icon.

On the command prompt write following command.

```
sudo apt install ttf-mscorefonts-installer
```

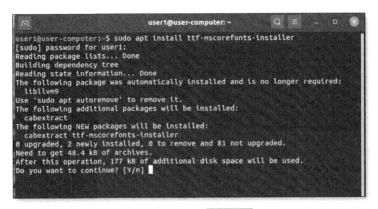

Provide password and press Enter Key.

Follow the steps

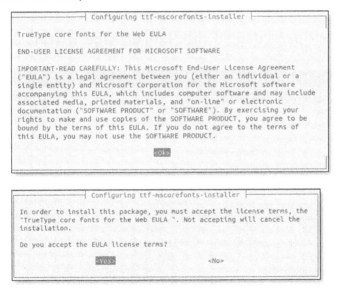

Set default fonts

Once fonts are installed. Click Writer icon on the dash bar to open the LibreWriter.

Click **Tools** from the main menu and select **options**.

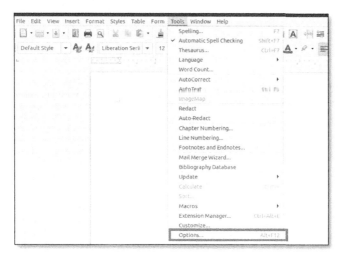

In left pane double click **LibreOffice writer**. Select **Basic**

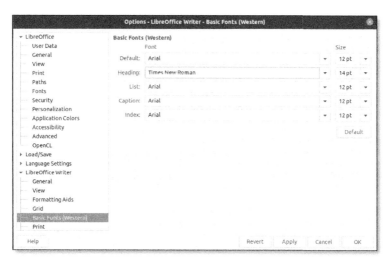

fonts.

On right Pane change the default font to Arial and heading to Times new roman.

Change Icon style

Click **LibreOffice** on left pane and select **View**

Change **Icon style** to **Breeze** from drop down menu.

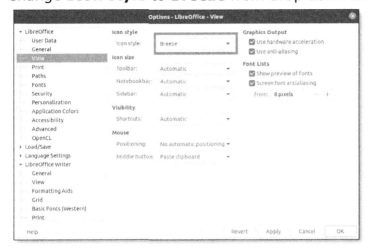

Change file format to docx

Double click Load /Save in the left pane. Select **General**.

Change **Always save as** to **Word 2007-365(*.docx)**
using drop down menu

Press OK.

Change user interface

Click **View** from the menu and select **User interface**.

Select **tabbed**.

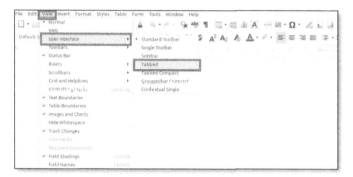

The final Writer will look like bellow

Printed in Great Britain
by Amazon

21175122R00068